Send Him A Signal

61 Secrets For Indicating Interest And Attracting The Attention Of Higher Quality Men

By Bruce Bryans

www.BruceBryans.com

Legal Disclaimer

Although the information in this book may be very useful, it is sold with the understanding that neither the author nor the publisher is engaged in presenting specific psychological, emotional, or sexual advice. Nor is anything in this book intended to be a diagnosis, prescription, recommendation, or cure for any specific kind of psychological, emotional, or sexual problem. Each person has unique needs and this book cannot take these individual differences into account.

This book is copyright © 2015 by Bruce Bryans with all rights reserved. It is <u>illegal</u> to copy, distribute, or create derivative works from this book in whole or in part or to contribute to the copying, distribution, or creating of derivative works of this book.

No part of this report may be reproduced or transmitted in any form whatsoever, electronic, or mechanical, including photocopying, recording, or by any informational storage or retrieval system without expressed written, dated and signed permission from the author.

Table of Contents

Introduction 1

Chapter 1 - Out With The Girls: Social Strategies for Standing Out and Catching His Eye 9

Chapter 2 - Out On Your Own: Subtle Moves to Entice Him towards You 25

Chapter 3 - Change Your Attitude: The Keys to Removing Your Invisible Anti-Guy Barrier 53

Chapter 4 - Reel Him In: Simple Tips for Being Irresistible and Securing His Interest 69

Chapter 5 - Love At First Sight: How to Captivate Him With a Flawless First Impression 77

Chapter 6 - How Men Think: Understanding the Mind of an Interested Man 89

Introduction

Contrary to popular belief, men aren't as simple as they make us out to be. Yes, we tend to be a bit simple in terms of our wants and needs, but when it comes to the challenge of attracting women you'll find that even the simplest of men become calculating strategists in order to achieve their goals.

So while we are simple in many areas, when it comes to securing the affections of a woman, we're far more complex than you can imagine. So complex in fact, those men who have a bit more experience with women learn very quickly how to maximize their chances of success (and minimize their losses) with a woman by developing an intricate behavior-reading system that tells them whether or not a woman is either highly approachable or highly interested in them.

But why do men need this system? Well, because it helps us to increase the chances of courting a woman who's really into us while vastly lowering the risk of being rejected.

There have been times that I've approached women and from those approaches I've found myself in some pretty fun relationships. There have been other times that I've approached women and found myself on the receiving end of some nasty rejections, and even then it's all been good fun. But one thing I did learn better over time was how to figure out a woman's level of interest in me. This was an extremely important skill to develop because as I interacted with women I was able to minimize rejections and maximize success with the special ladies who had higher levels of interest (which eventually led me to the woman I'm now happily married to).

But during this whole dating experience there was *one* thing that I learned that heavily influenced both the eagerness and tenacity of how I pursued a woman. It was that the courting process is definitely a two way street. A lot of women expect men to figure things out and "take a hint" when in actuality they haven't been giving the *right* hints at all. Some women might even think that they shouldn't have to give any hints; believing in the false notion that if a guy is interested he'll take the risk and make a move. Sure, you can wait on your Mr. McDreamy to finally man-up and ask you out, but why not make life just a little easier on the guy and send him a signal that he can recognize.

Men with even a hint of confidence and at least *some* experience with women will develop the ability to tell if a woman is interested in them or not. This is why learning how to indicate your interest <u>in a way that men recognize</u> is important. It helps you to weed out guys with lower levels of interest (something no woman wants) from guys with higher levels of interest. If you signal your interest to a guy and he's interested in you (and doesn't suffer from debilitating social anxiety) he's more likely to pick up on your signals and pursue you.

So whether it's a perfect stranger you've just met or a handsome acquaintance that you'd like to spend some alone time with, learning to send a guy the right signals might be the missing ingredient to your courting strategy.

Women With Options Get What They Want

You might be asking yourself: What does it benefit a woman to make herself more attractive and approachable to men? Well, aside from making it even just a bit easier to attract a great guy into your life, becoming more approachable to men in general will help you to avoid *desperation*.

If you're barely approached by men at all or they barely notice or take interest in you, it's going to be a lot more difficult for you to learn how to filter out the players and time-wasters from the men who are genuinely interested in a committed relationship. It's even going to be a lot *more* difficult for you to say "NO" to those guys who aren't interested in a relationship simply because you won't have that inner confidence that says, *"Hey, pass on this guy, he's not worth it. You know you can do better than this loser."*

Women with options don't have to settle or act needy and desperate with men. They trust that if they're not being treated with respect and value, they can easily attract another guy sooner than later. The sad truth is, if you feel really unconfident about when the next guy is going to show up or if one will show up at all, you may find yourself in desperate situations with men that you *know* aren't right for you.

A woman might get that *gut* feeling that tells her when a guy is going to waste her time. But if she's unconfident about her odds in the dating market, she's more likely to "see where this thing goes" and waste her time. Sure, she might grow to like him and even end up deeply attached to him emotionally, etc., but it always boils down to one question that every woman in a lukewarm relationship or friends-with-benefits dating situation has to ask herself: *Can I really do better than this?*

Think of it this way, if you're in more of a position where you can pick, choose, and refuse men, you won't have to *settle* for Mr. Wrongs or even Mr. Just-This-One-Time. The reality is, women who don't know how to gain the attention of the kind of men they want may find themselves doing all sorts of desperate things to both find and keep any willing bodied man that shows up. What's more is that because of the kind of men this sort of behavior attracts, a woman may find herself struggling with one dead-end relationship after another or worse, men who are only interested in using her for sexual gratification.

Different Women Send Different Signs

Different women will do very different things when interested in a guy. An introverted woman may become even shyer and closed up around a guy friend she's attracted to or even around a complete stranger that has caught her eye. On the other hand, a more extroverted woman may become overly catty and even mean-natured with her teasing towards a guy friend she's attracted to or a hot and handsome stranger. So as you can see, different women do very different things when they see a guy they like or when they experience a natural attraction towards a guy friend.

This is the reality.

But here's another reality…

Most men have no idea that this is the case *unless* they have had considerable experience with the opposite sex.

Back in college, before I had a firm (firmer?) grasp on women's behaviors, I've known girls who had wild crushes on me but did nothing but go out of their way to make my life difficult (the extroverts). On the other hand, I've also known girls who would act indifferent and almost try to disappear when I was around only to find out *way* later that they were smitten by me (the introverts). This experience is not unique to me. It happens and has happened to just about every reasonably attractive man on this planet in some form or fashion.

And it is frustrating.

All men subconsciously seek out certain indicators that tell them whether or not a woman is *okay* to pursue. We tend to want to mitigate as much risk as possible when it comes to romantic pursuits in order to protect the fragile male ego or the priceless masculine reputation. If you're an extrovert and you choose to mask your insecurities (because you *really* do like him) by acting arrogant or difficult, unless he's experienced enough with female behavior, he's going to think that you're definitely not interested in him. On the other hand, if you're an introvert and you choose to mask your insecurities by closing up, being unsociable, or acting aloof, you're going to come off cold and again, uninterested.

The difficulty for men is gaining enough

experience with the opposite sex in order to pick up on these counterintuitive behaviors and act in spite of what the situation looks like on the outside. But by the time a man does gain that experience, he might have missed a thousand opportunities to pursue and court a woman who had a high interest in him. Even you, as a woman can probably recognize those missed opportunities with men who just did not "get it" and you were forced to move your affections onto another Mr. McDreamy who was a bit more astute to the wiles of a woman.

I say all this to bring home the point that though different women act differently when they're interested in a man, in general, men tend to read signs of romantic interest in a very uniform way. Yes, you can "be yourself" and maybe your Mr. McDreamy has gained enough experience with women to pick up on your brand of craziness, but don't count on it.

Place the odds in your favor by adopting a seduction strategy that speaks *directly* to the masculine subconscious. If you're an introvert, shutting down or acting bizarre might work if your Mr. McDreamy is unusually relentless in his pursuit of a woman, but like I said before, such an occurrence is more of a long shot in today's highly competitive dating arena.

In a landscape where the number of single women far outnumbers single men, men, unfortunately for women, have a ton of options in how they can approach the dating process. Learning how to send the right kinds of men the right kinds of signals will help you to place the odds more in your favor.

And that, my friend, is what this book is about.

What to Expect From This Book

Men want to give chase, but don't want to waste their time and energy on women whose interest in them is zero to non-existent. Women want men to chase but don't want to have to hold a man's hand in the seduction process for fear of appearing needy, desperate, or simply undesirable to men among their peers.

This is a frustrating dilemma that affects both men and women.

So how do you show a guy you're interested and become more approachable without doing all the work yourself (and thereby ruining everyone's fun)?

Well, that's what you're going to find out in the following pages.

Now, keep in mind that the advice I espouse within these pages are tailored towards single women looking to make themselves more approachable to men they don't know (yet) and also to single women who want to use subtle techniques to let an acquaintance know that they're interested in him. Also consider that the advice may seem one-sided because <u>this book is for women</u>. In my books for men I give them the other side of the equation, helping them to "man up" and go after what they really want instead of waiting for things to fall into their laps. I pull no punches with the guys and I won't do so with you.

I also don't intend to insult your intelligence either. I'm fully aware that the best and obvious way to let a man know you're interested in him is to walk up to him, strike up a conversation, tell him you think he's attractive, and then ask him out for a cup of coffee (or something just as casual). If all women did this dating would be a lot simpler for both men and women. But this is not the way MOST women want to begin a courtship with a man. And believe it or not, not *all* men want to begin a courtship this way either. So with that said, this book was written for women who want to indicate their interest to a man without completely leading the interaction or being entirely overt about it.

Lastly, though this book will help you to take just a little more initiative in the courting process, in no way, shape, or form am I advocating that a woman bend over backwards just to get a guy's attention. Men are hard-wired by nature to pursue women and they want to do just that. However, due to social changes, cultural conventions, and a highly politically correct society, many men have taken a more *passive* or *risk-averse* way in expressing romantic interest in a woman.

This book isn't about making women more aggressive in the dating and courtship rituals, it's about making them smarter in order to place the odds in their favor. It's also about helping women to help the men who don't have a clue. And as you should have realized by now…most men *really* don't have a clue.

So if you have an open mind and you're eager to learn the *right* signals that men watch for in an interested women, let's dive into the meat of the book, shall we?

Chapter 1

Out With The Girls:
Social Strategies for Standing Out and Catching His Eye

1

A man will avoid pursuing a beautiful stranger if she's surrounded by a large group of her girlfriends. Keep your group small if you wish to coax a handsome observer to make an approach.

Unless he's had a few drinks (liquid courage) or has developed an abnormal amount of self-confidence, no man in his right mind is going to approach you alone if you're surrounded by a large group of your girlfriends. For the man of average or even slightly above average confidence, a group of two to three women is the limit in which he will "man up" and approach you. If he has less than average confidence you can forget about him approaching you unless it's just you and *maybe* one other woman with you.

Large groups of women are intimidating for most men. Groups of two or three are preferable because it makes it easier for a man to avoid the awkwardness of having to "extract" you from your large group in order to get to know you in a more one-on-one setting. Being in a smaller group also relieves him of the pressure of having to charm your entire group, especially since he may already be stepping outside of his comfort zone just to charm you.

The added benefit of being in a smaller group is

that it creates a better situation for attracting decent, quality guys. Keep in mind that men who have significantly more experience seducing women for sexual conquest alone are sometimes *more* likely to approach larger groups of women. While being in a smaller group won't do anything to dissuade Mr. Wrong from trying his hand, it certainly won't be a deterrent to Mr. Right either.

2

The woman whose girlfriend doubles as a personal guard dog will ensure that her social escapades are free from both unwanted AND *wanted* male attention. Either leave her at home or keep her restrained if you do not wish such a fate to befall you.

All men who have tried to chat with a beautiful woman in some sort of group setting have experienced "the man-repellant friend" of the girl they were enamored with. Once again, while your man-repellant friend may be useful for shutting down slimy guys she also won't do you any favors when a potential Mr. Right tries to infiltrate your group. She's a risk, a high risk that reduces the odds of men approaching you.

Now, you love your girlfriends and that's understandable, so you won't always want to ditch the ones who might be well trained man-away every time you go out. The best thing you can do is to tell her (or them) beforehand that if a man approaches you to refrain from being difficult with him. And even more so, let her know that if a man tries to isolate you for a conversation, do not try to pull you away from him.

Be clear about this because some of your girlfriends might simply not know that they habitually scare men away because of their body language or behavior. Also keep in mind that jealousy and overprotectiveness might also be a reason why your girlfriends might act this way.

You're doing yourself a big disservice if you use your girlfriends to keep men at bay. If you always use your girlfriends as a "shield" you'll never learn for yourself how to filter out the good guys from the slime. Learning how to quickly tell the difference between a man who is genuinely interested in you from a man who just wants another notch on his bedpost is an invaluable skill for a woman to have. Don't be afraid to socially interact with all types of men so that you can learn the differences between them for yourself.

3

Sticking too close to guy friends will result in a hapless evening. Though competitive by nature, a man will not encroach upon what he thinks is another man's girlfriend. Refrain

from tagging along with that which readily repels men – *other* men.

This one should be common sense, but I figure it won't hurt to mention it here. If you bring a man or a group of men out with you...do not expect *other* men to approach you. The probability of a guy pursuing you when a group of guys are circling you and your friends like sharks surrounding a school of mackerel is zero to none.

Even if a guy is really interested in you, if he sees men with you he might assume that you're either dating one of them or that it's just too much trouble. It's extremely difficult for a man to get to know you if he has to deal with your protective male friend or some other friend-zoned guy you continue to torture by bringing him along on your girl's night out. Don't bring your guy friends if you want to make *new* guy friends. Got it?

Now, you might think that having men out with you is a safety buffer of some kind and that their presence can lead to meeting *new* guys. In some cases, this can be true. Having guy friends hang out with you can lead to some great introductions so long as your guy friends don't mind introducing you to their friends.

This is based on the strong assumption that the guys you go out with are not romantically interested in you in any way, because if they are and you continue to hang out with them in social settings where *other* men abound, they're nothing but deadweight to you. Be careful of going out with guy friends who are secretly attracted to or in love with you (also known as the "friend-zoned"). They're useless when it comes to meeting new guys.

4

Men require a clear exit should their boldness end in rejection. No man wants to look ridiculous in his effort to make a hasty escape.

A great way to lower the risks of rejection for a guy is to situate yourself in such a way as so he has a clear way of escape if you deny his advances. If approaching and interacting with you looks like a mantrap he's not going to take that chance. Guys will assess how easily accessible you are and how fast they can slip away should things go sour. You want to stand or sit in places that allow him to move in and out without many obstacles. In fact, men tend to prioritize approaches where they don't have to leave the way they came or where they don't have to leave empty-handed.

For example, four girls hidden away in some corner of the room, nursing drinks and chatting with each other might appear to be a mantrap to some guys. How so? Well, you're sitting far away in some corner where it will be ridiculously obvious to all that he was rejected if he approaches you, is not offered a seat, and ends up leaving the way he came.

How do you make it look like less of a mantrap? First, keep your group small, as I've already mentioned.

Secondly, keep an open space next to you. This could be an empty seat or even just a space for him to stand so it at least looks like he could quickly "blend" in with the surroundings and engage with you. Do not situate yourself in places that force him to leave unrewarded or as if he was very unwelcomed.

Consider a restaurant bar scenario for instance. It would be a lot less risky if a guy can pull up to the bar, sit on the free seat next to you, and say "hi" as he orders his drink than if he has to tap you on the shoulder to get your attention and stand behind you (while you and a friend are seated) since all the seats are taken. A seat next to you means that he won't be intrusive (by tapping you on the shoulder) and being able to access the bar means he can at least walk away with a drink, which will help to mask his rejection. In other words…he won't have to walk away empty-handed. Yes, he got rejected, but hey…at least he got to order a drink (his "reward") and say "hi" to an attractive woman in the process.

Giving a man a clear exit usually presents a challenge for most women because females in general prioritize safety and the "keep away" game in social settings where men are more likely to engage the opposite sex. This is understandable, but as I keep mentioning, playing it safe doesn't place the odds in your favor.

5

The ardent admirer cannot resist a beautiful woman who emanates a zest for life. The irresistible woman is one who enjoys more the merriments of her social outings than the attention of men.

Girls aren't the only ones who want to have fun. Men want to have just as much fun (perhaps even more) than you do. And there's nothing more inviting than an attractive group of women who appear as if their having fun is a higher priority than trying to impress men (or other women). If your level of fun is highly dependent on the quality of the music, whether your high heels hold up or not, or the amount of men that approach you, you're handicapping yourself.

Men watch for signs in a woman's behavior that will give him a good idea of just how difficult she might be to deal with. If a woman's personal happiness and enjoyment looks like it requires far too many factors, a man is less likely to approach. This is why having a good time with or without your friends and regardless of the circumstances or venue is a great way to make yourself much more approachable to great guys.

While you might want to prioritize being more approachable to great guys overall (you do this by adjusting your social behaviors), you do not want to make it your sole focus every time you go out. I know it sounds very counterintuitive, but that's the nature of attraction. High-quality men *love* engaging with women who can have fun whether or not they're attracting the attention of the men around them. Trust me on this.

As I mention in my book, <u>The 7 Irresistible Qualities Men Want In A Woman</u>, high-quality men are usually excellent judges of character, and they tend to quickly evaluate whether or not a woman is worth the effort based not merely on her appearance, but also on what her behavior says about her <u>character</u>. When a man like this observes a woman in a social setting, freely expressing herself, and having a good time regardless of what men think of her, he realizes (albeit subconsciously) that:

1. Her self-esteem must be high since she is not a slave to the attention of men.

2. If she's not a slave to the attention of men then she might make for a loyal girlfriend someday, and…

3. Approaching her won't end in insult or rudeness since a woman with high-self esteem would also have a higher amount of respect for others.

Yes, relationship-minded men, who are less likely to waste a woman's time, think in this way. And unfortunately, most women probably aren't even aware of it.

6

After you silently introduce yourself to him with your eyes, isolate yourself so as to encourage your ardent admirer to give chase.

If you so happen to make some positive eye contact with a guy you find attractive, a great way to make him less risk averse is to isolate yourself for a period of time. What this means is that once you make some positive exchange between you and your perfect stranger, instead of hanging around your group of girlfriends move to another location that might be a bit closer to him but not completely out of sight from your safety net – your friends. It's okay to stay within viewing distance of your group, but don't be afraid to branch off for a few minutes nearer to or at least within your perfect stranger's line of sight.

Remember, you're trying to appeal to the male's natural desire to *pursue*. Men know that women find a lot of safety in numbers, but they also know that a woman is less likely to be rude or over-critical of them when she's alone. By isolating yourself after making positive eye contact a man subconsciously gets the message that you're now in perfect position to be pursued. If you position yourself accordingly and after at least five minutes of isolation he doesn't make a move…return to your station. You want a guy who takes advantage of the opportunities that life throws at him, not one who wanes and waffles when what he wants is literally right in front of him.

7

Every woman, though unknown to her, plays a role among her group... Allow your function to be that of the "cool one" should your temperament permit. Such a woman is the most genuine of her friends, thus she draws the attention of many ardent admirers.

Being the "cool one" in your group means that men find you extremely easy to get along with. You understand men on a level that your peers don't. You know that they want respect, admiration from women (and other men), and that what they really enjoy is the thrill of the hunt. I've met groups of women where there weren't any "cool ones."

Being cool is simply about being humble and affable. You don't see men as the enemy or even a target, and you enjoy the process of being approached by men and interacting with them simply for who they are. In short, being the "cool one" means that you're the most *genuine* girl in your group.

I know this sounds sort of cheesy, but cool girls are

approached by more authentic men than the most dolled up women at a social gathering. The quality of the men that approach and connect with her will be far superior to the kind of men that pursue a woman who is all show but no substance. Like attracts like, so if you want to connect with more authentic, sincere guys…consider learning how to understand and socialize with men in order to increase your confidence to become the "cool one."

8

Every woman, though unknown to her, plays a role among her group... Allow your function to be that of the "fun one" should your temperament permit. Such a woman is the most exuberant of her friends, thus she also draws the attention of many attractive admirers.

If you're a bit more extroverted and have the confidence to back it up, you might want to consider being the "fun one." While the "cool girl" is the girl in the group that helps guys to feel less awkward or intrusive around her and her friends once introductions are made, the "fun one" is the girl in the group that makes those introductions. She's the one who goes out of her way to ensure that her girlfriends are having a good time and will usually be the link in her group that gets them out of the "girl's club only" mode into the "let's meet some cool guys" mode.

Men LOVE the "fun one." I clearly remember my friends and I becoming ecstatic when we saw an attractive group of girls at a social gathering and saw that there was indeed, a "fun one" amidst the group. We knew that in order to infiltrate the group and meet everyone, all we had to do was connect with the "fun one." It was a flawless strategy simply because the "fun one" would almost *insist* that we meet her friends and that we all should hang out together.

Naturally, just like some guys, some women have social anxieties and trepidations that make them *seem* very unapproachable. Often, it's not that these women don't want men to connect with them; it's just that they give off a nervous, negative energy that makes them seem like a high-risk pursuit. The "fun one" on the other hand is usually the most extroverted girl in the group. Her smiles, giggling, and social mannerisms give off a positive energy that tells men that she's open to meeting new people and having some good, clean fun with them.

Now, just so there's no confusion, keep in mind that when I say the "fun one" I don't mean that a woman has to be the life of the party necessarily. Being "fun" simply means that men love your confident, sociable, and fearless energy, and it makes you super easy to approach because of all the positivity you radiate. The "fun" one doesn't have to make a spectacle out of herself or be obnoxious or loud. She can be fun without losing her class and dignity.

9

Be wary of girlfriends who monopolize all male attention. If one of them is an aggressive flirt, she will ensure that men will never know of your existence. And if another's beauty clearly eclipses your own, the end result of your social outings will always prove fruitless.

Do not keep company with girlfriends that suck all the attention of men in their direction. It might not make sense at first, but if being more approachable to men is your highest priority you'd be better off limiting how often you hang out with girlfriends who make it their priority to steal all the attention.

Whether they do this by being extra flirtatious or augmenting their appearance in order to draw the stares of men in their direction is inconsequential. If you want to avoid an evening of watching your girlfriend flirt and finesse her way into the hearts of guys whom you wished knew you were alive, limit your time spent with her.

Now, some women might think that if a guy thought their friend was more attractive than they were, that's fine; or that they don't think that having a friend who gets approached by men more often than they themselves is perfectly okay. Listen, I'm only here to give you the ugly truth, and the truth of this point is as ugly as it gets.

If a man has never met you or your girlfriend before, but your girlfriend is either more physically attractive and/or flirtatious than you are...it is highly probable that he will focus his attention on your girlfriend. It might not be because he finds you dull, unattractive, or even stuck-up. He will focus his attention on your girlfriend simply because she *appears* to be a lower risk and/or higher reward pursuit.

So what's the moral of the story? Do not go out to meet guys with women that *you know* are far more physically attractive than you are. You can be as beautiful and mysterious as the moon, but if your girlfriend is the sun...you'll vanish.

I do acknowledge the fact that there's no single marker of physical beauty, but your cumulative experience while out with your girlfriend will clearly tell you if the higher quality men always choose her over you, leaving you stuck to interact with his less-than-dreamy wingman...if he even has one. With that said, if you constantly surround yourself with women who are far more attractive than you are, you're not placing the odds in your favor at all. You've been warned.

10

The sweet, girlish laughter of women serenades the masculine ear and lures in the most curious of men. To a single man the sound is as sweet and tantalizing as honeycomb to a bear.

This may seem strange at first, but hear me out. A lot of guys are attracted to girlish laughter. It's cute, it's feminine, and it registers deeply within the masculine subconscious. Modest, girlish laughter (not garrulous outbursts) is like catnip for men. Men love to see women having fun in some capacity, and the sweet sound of warm, girlish laughter can, in the least, pique the interest of men within an earshot of you and your group.

I know you might be thinking that this all sounds like utter nonsense, but trust me when I say that at social gatherings, especially ones with large amounts of people, the sound of girlish laughter can draw men in closer to you and your friends faster than you can imagine.

Chapter 2

Out On Your Own:
Subtle Moves to Entice Him towards You

11

The handsome observer watches the facial expressions of the woman that has caught his eye. If her facial expressions appear to be cold or surly, he may deem her as unfit to approach.

A lot of women make it impossible for men to approach them simply by the look they wear on their faces. Men are usually watching you <u>when you're least aware that they are</u>. This means that by the time you make eye contact and smile with that hot guy leaving Starbucks with his order, he's already seen you walk through the door with a scowl on your face and figured that you're either having a bad day or you're just not friendly. To him, the eye contact and smile you gave him might come off as nothing more than you trying to be nice to him since you caught him looking in your direction.

You see, everyone has a "resting" face; that face that they wear when they're not feeling any particular emotion at all. If your resting face is a pout, a serious glare, or a listless gaze of indifference, you're not doing yourself any favors. Because guys will, quite often, notice you way before you notice them, you can improve your approachability by leaps and bounds by merely changing your resting face to a more positive one.

I should note that you don't have to have a smoky or sultry look to make guys notice you in a more positive light. Trying to wear a "sexy", model-like facial expression might actually work against you as well, especially if you don't know how to pull it off without looking fake. What guys want to see in general is that coolness factor. He needs to glance in your direction and think, *"Wow, she looks cool enough to walk over and talk to"* or, *"She looks fun and relaxed, like she's easy to talk to."* Men aren't expecting you to act in a way that seems fake or forced. All they want to see are positive signs that communicate openness towards social interaction with other human beings.

12

A woman would be wise to consider how her attitude affects those around her; especially to the types of men she is most interested in attracting.

Keep aware of the kind of vibe you're putting out there, especially to men. This has to do with the kind of energy you put out, and by energy I mean *attitude in action*. The wrong vibe will net you the wrong kind of attention from the wrong guys while the right vibe can do just the opposite.

I mention this because of the claims a lot of women often make about the kinds of men they'd like to meet but fail to do so. They'd like to attract the attention of certain kinds of men but their social vibes say otherwise.

For example, if you're always over-the-top and hyper, some guys are going to find you overwhelming. There's nothing wrong with this if you don't mind *not* attracting the attention of men with calmer dispositions. Yes, opposites do attract, but unless chance or circumstance drives them together a guy like this is not going to go out of his way to say "Hello."

Whether you believe it or not, you're sending out vibes every single time you go out into the world to interact with other people. Everyone sends them out. In fact, I'm sure that you've even picked up the vibes from people around you.

For example, you may be in a room full of people but then you see this guy watching you from across the room. He may even approach you and introduce himself. After a very short conversation (one that you end), he leaves, and you turn to your girlfriend and say, *"Yikes, I don't know about that guy. He has this creepy vibe about him."*

Imagine that. Some guy you've never met before but in a short amount of time leaves you with the impression that he's "creepy." Just how a woman can pick up the kind of vibe a man is sending out, so do men. And since you're sending out vibes regardless, you might as well work on sending out the right kinds.

13

A look of boredom will do nothing to tempt the ardent admirer to risk meeting you. Therefore, it does not benefit a woman to wear a look of boredom unless she wishes to attract the attention of a Lothario. The Lothario will see her as just another fun challenge, and she will never be sure of his true intentions.

This point is a perfect example of the energy management concept I mentioned earlier. Having a look of boredom is a sure way to keep some guys at bay. Admittedly though, some men might see your boredom as an opportunity to "make your day" by giving you the pleasure of a chance encounter with themselves. Again, betting on being approached by guys like this is a long shot since only men with higher levels of charm and confidence (i.e., those more experienced with women) are going to take on the challenge of piquing your interest or putting a smile on your jaded face.

To men, a bored feminine face is perceived as indifference or apathy. It's not warm or inviting and makes most men think that the costs of pursuing you far outweigh the benefits.

14

Excellent posture is as rare among women as it is among men. Even more rare is a woman who knows how to employ her posture in a welcoming way. While flawless posture increases a woman's attractiveness, friendly posture increases her approachability.

The first impression a man gets of your posture says a lot to him. Good posture goes a long way towards making a man take extra notice of you. Why? Well, because good posture…no, excellent posture, is uncommon. That stuff that your mom, teachers, and grandmother taught you as a young girl *really* does matter.

Sitting up straight makes a woman look dignified and graceful and does wonders for how her breasts appear (ALL men assess the shapely assets of a woman they're interested in – get over it). And while a crossed pair of legs looks great on a woman, a crossed pair of arms does not.

Good posture also promotes good health and makes you appear more fertile, and therefore more attractive. Anything that's good for making babies is sexy, and men can't help but at least take notice of a woman with both queenly and friendly posture. My suggestion? Grab a good book on female body language or etiquette if you think you need to improve your posturing habits.

15

Loud environments do not make for easy introductions between two admirers. If she wishes to converse intimately with her perfect gentleman it would benefit a woman to avoid such places.

Ever tried to have a conversation with the opposite sex at a loud party or concert? If your experience was anything like mine, I'm sure it was an effort in futility. Loud places are not great environments for making introductions and having conversations with perfect strangers. It's weird, it's awkward, and everyone leaves feeling just a little bit more stupid for having to shout sentences like, "I SAID…IT'S NICE TO MEET YOU!" Some guys would never go out of their way to meet a woman in an environment that required them to shout like an imbecile.

Also keep in mind that for guys there's the added level of unintended creepiness where he has to lean in close to your ears just to get you to hear what he's saying. This might be fine if you're already friends or acquaintances (or if you secretly want him that close to you), but a guy you don't know can get really self-conscious about accidentally grazing his lips against your earlobe in a hopeless attempt to introduce himself.

But if you do find yourself at a function that makes conversation impossible, try to spend a bit more time in a less raucous spot within the venue. The benefit here is that the guys that actually *want* to have casual conversations with the opposite sex will gravitate towards this area as well.

16

Making a woman laugh, especially one a man has just met, is no easy feat. The astute woman, knowing that her brave pursuer has taken on a great challenge, will at the least, indulge his humor.

I know some women cringe at the idea of laughing at a man's jokes even when he's not funny. But, as much as I hate to admit it, yes...men love making women laugh and smile. Think about it. Men study books on flirting with women, picking up women, and pleasing women in bed. Why? Well, it's because we want to please women. Pleasing women pleases our egos. And nothing rips a man of his confidence faster than a woman who's not laughing at his best material.

If he's not that funny you don't have to be over-the-top, laughing hysterically just to make him feel good about himself. All you have to do is *indulge* him. If he throws a quick quip your way give him at least a chuckle and toss something witty and/or flirtatious right back at him.

You're not being dishonest by giving him a smile or laugh; you're simply sending him a socially acceptable form of communication that you think he's interesting. Sometimes a man may gauge your level of interest simply based on how well his brand of humor affects you. If the jokes don't land (on either side) then sometimes that's a sign that there's very little chemistry.

17

Retreating from the action gives the handsome observer a chance to detect and pursue you. It also gives you the equal opportunity to assess his resolve to meet you as well.

If you're in a particularly busy or bustling location that makes casual conversation difficult you might want to pull away from the action for a while. It often happens where a guy will notice an attractive woman but the area is far too crowded or socially suffocating to do any sort of introductions. This piece of advice comes with a caveat, however.

While you want to get away from the action, don't retreat out of sight. You want to be able to be seen by the crowd (where men are sure to be) but not necessarily a part of it. This is an excellent strategy because you can get a good sense of just how interested a guy really is if he takes the initiative to leave a busy location just to get to know you.

18

A smile and a wave is one of the most direct signals of a woman's interest. Any man, even a shy one, will undoubtedly feel like a fool if he fails to act.

I have a confession. If you can effectively implement this one tactic you probably won't need to study the rest of this book. Why? Well, because any man with even the tiniest bit of intelligence (yes, we do exist) and confidence is going to *leap* at the opportunity to talk to a woman who makes eye contact, smiles at him, waves, and mimes the word "Hi".

You'll be even more effective if you can make eye contact, smile, wave, and mime "Hi" while doing a cute and subtle, girlish tilt of the head at the same time. You know, the one where you tilt your head and expose one side of your neck. Yes, that one!

19

After his approach, the bold pursuer will *need* immediate feedback as to where he stands with a woman. By helping him break the ice, she can increase his confidence and thus stoke the fiery coals of chemistry.

Helping a man to break the ice means that you're engaging him *enthusiastically*. It means that if a guy had the courage to approach you, instead of making him do all the work, you reciprocate by asking him interesting questions in order to get to know him. Don't just stand or sit there responding to him as if you were on some sort of job interview. Meet him halfway and engage him.

Men want to know almost immediately how well they're doing as they're getting to know you. And one of the best ways they receive that instant feedback is by how engrossed you are in the conversation. A great way to improve in this area of communication is to learn the fine art of small talk. You don't have to be a master conversationalist to communicate positively with men, but it's a lot easier to create chemistry with a woman who at least knows how to make small talk fun and interesting.

20

The handsome observer is likely to consider a woman wearing headphones as one who wishes to be left alone. And being the gentleman that he is, he will grant her this wish.

Headphones on a woman are akin to a billboard sign on her forehead that reads: PLEASE DO NOT SPEAK TO ME. A man reads this message loud and clear and, unless he is driven by an insatiable urge to speak to you, he will acquiesce your request to leave you alone. Your headphones are merely another obstacle that will stop guys from approaching you. Place the odds in your favor and ditch them.

21

The handsome observer is also likely to consider a woman engaged with her smartphone as one who wishes to be left alone. And again, being the gentleman that he is, he will grant her this wish.

I'm sure I don't have to go into excruciating detail as to how having your face glued to a smartphone turns off even the most interested of men, right? Most men, with even a reasonable amount of social etiquette, will be discouraged from pursuing you if you appear completely engaged with your smartphone.

Whether you're patiently waiting on a text or absorbed in a game of Angry Birds doesn't matter. Once a guy sees your head in your phone he'll be less likely to disturb you. Remember that your smartphone is a tool that should make your life easier. Don't let it hinder you from improving your chances of meeting a nice guy.

22

High-quality men assess a woman's relationship potential based on her social behavior. To court the attention of such men, a woman would be wise to treat people with overflowing kindness.

Because a man will observe a woman closely to figure out whether or not she's worth the effort, you might want to consider treating others with excessive kindness. If a man observes you treating the staff of a local eatery with warmth and kindness he's less likely to think that an interaction with you will end badly. Even should someone affront you, if you handle it with grace and poise, you're also more likely to attract his adoration than his disdain.

A woman who can rise above the petty-mindedness of others is highly attractive to good men, men of high character. Now, I'm not advocating that you become a pushover and not defend your personal boundaries should you be disrespected. What I am saying is that it benefits you greatly to show an extra amount of kindness to others, acting from a place of grace and benevolence, especially towards strangers, because it will attract the *right* kind of attention.

As I mentioned before, high-quality men are excellent judges of character. If a man observes you ripping the waiter a new one simply because he mixed up your order he's not going to think you're a strong woman who knows what she wants. He's going to think you're impatient, rude, and probably high maintenance.

Sure, it's a lot easier to give someone a piece of your mind when they affront you, but as with all things communicative, it's not *what* you say that matters sometimes but *how* you say it. You can put someone in their place if they disrespect you without coming across like one of those hell-on-high-heels types.

Quality, relationship-minded men pay more attention to a woman's behavior than the average guy. So be sure to repay the kindness of others with kindness, and as you grow in tolerance, learn to *extend* your kindness to those who may offend you as well.

23

It is inevitable for a woman to receive unwanted attention from male observers. But, if she can reject these men with kindness, she ensures that the hopes of her desired admirer will not be completely dashed.

In a larger social setting there's always the chance of a woman receiving both wanted and unwanted attention from men. Because of this, if you so happen to get unwanted attention from a guy be careful of how you reject him. Many women have no idea that guys are watching how they treat *other* men when they're not interested.

When a guy observes you rejecting another guy his first thought will be that you might not be approachable and that his efforts might end in the same results. You can do nothing to change this thought. However, if his interest levels are high enough he might still want to get to know you depending on *how* you rejected the previous guy.

It says a lot about a woman if she can reject a man with both tact and kindness. It takes a lot of guts to approach a woman you don't know or to ask an attractive acquaintance out on a date. You don't have to sugarcoat your rejection since it's better that a man knows off the bat that you're not interested. But even in your denial you should at least treat him with respect and dignity. The ability to do so will speak volumes about your character to other interested men.

24

If she has done a masterful job at piquing a man's curiosity through eye contact, a woman can increase his window of opportunity to take pursuit by closing the distance.

In environments where a lot of people clamor together it may be a bit more difficult for your Mr. McDreamy to get close to you, especially if he's already engaged with a group of his own. In situations such as this one it might benefit a woman to get a little closer to her perfect stranger, especially if she's already done a good job of making positive eye contact with him.

Along with making it easier for a guy to interact with you, moving closer to him helps to draw the attention of his comrades. I've been in social situations where my friends brought it to my attention that a certain girl seemed to be trying to get my attention. Because men are always on the lookout for interested women, a guy's friends can be useful tools for making your presence known so long as it's done with finesse.

25

A gentle collision with a beautiful woman gives a man an excuse to interrupt and initiate conversation with her.

This tactic obviously depends on the kind of social setting you're in. If you're in a location where you have to move between people, if there's a guy you find attractive who's been making eye contact with you, you might want to consider bumping or brushing past him as you move from one point to another.

The reason I mention doing this only *after* you've made some positive eye contact is that it will solidify your interest in him, which will reduce any concerns he has of being rejected by you. Bumping or brushing against a guy you haven't made eye contact with might end in a wasted opportunity, especially if girls have been bumping past him the entire time.

I'll admit that this isn't a flawless strategy because if your Mr. McDreamy is too shy or lacks even a reasonable amount of confidence, he won't take the hint (eye contact) or even take the opportunity (bumping past him) to speak to you. This sort of social tactic works best on a handsome stranger who is both confident and interested in meeting you or an interested acquaintance who is at least somewhat familiar with you already.

26

The dance floor makes excellent hunting grounds for drunken gropers and pick-up artists. Limit your time spent there if you wish to lower the chances of encountering such men.

If you're at a party, try not to spend your entire night on the dance floor. I'm not saying *not* to dance the night away and have fun every once and a while, but do keep in mind that this isn't an optimal strategy for meeting the *best* guys at such venues. So while dancing may help you to feel less anxious, you may only find yourself being approached by strange men who'd rather spend the night groping you than getting to know you. This is especially true of nightclubs, which are perhaps the most non-ideal place for meeting men who aren't just interested in hooking up.

27

Situate yourself near the places that have the highest traffic of handsome specimens.

Depending on the venue, with some astute observation you might be able to tell where the men tend to congregate or move around the most. Position yourself near this location (once it's not the bathroom obviously) if you want to be both seen by a higher concentration of guys as well as be in a prime position to make eye contact with a handsome stranger.

For example, at a cocktail event you may find that the cocktail bar itself tends to be a hotspot for men who are both coming and going. You don't have to situate yourself *at* the cocktail bar, but being near to it is far superior to hiding away in some dark corner, nursing your appletini. Standing in some dark corner of the room is only good if you're interested in meeting vampires and other weirdoes.

28

A moving target might be hard to hit, but a moving woman is even harder to hit on. Some women are unapproachable because they are simply uncatchable.

While it may be tempting to move quickly about your environment in order to meet and greet as many people as you can, at some point you might want to settle down. Even if you choose not to stay put for too long, at least have some sort of home base that you return to frequently so that guys can position themselves near your comings and goings.

You can be as much of a social butterfly as you want but if you flutter about *too quickly* you might miss the opportunity to be approached by those guys who are probably waiting for you to perch someplace long enough to meet you. It's very rare for a woman to be approached by a man who had to literally hunt her down and block her path just to talk to her.

29

Many interested shy guys have stood near an attractive woman while hopelessly trying to think of the perfect thing to say. Save such shy men from their endearing futility by throwing them a conversational bone.

If you notice an attractive man going out of his way to get your attention or get close to you (if you think he's trying to get close to you but you're not too sure, trust me...he's trying to get close to you), throw him a conversational bone. There are numerous conversation starters that may be appropriate and even low-risk depending on the venue.

The art of making small talk requires nothing more

than an observant eye and a willingness to be amicable. Compliment him, make a witty observation, or even ask him a question to get the ball rolling. While it may be nerve-wracking for some women to initiate a conversation with a man they don't know, their fears are groundless since most men will immediately take it as a compliment if a woman takes the initiative to strike up a conversation with them.

30

Often, cultural mores will heavily influence a man's boldness in regards to his pursuit of a woman. Because of this, variables such as time and location tend to dictate what a man might consider, "acceptable" social behavior. The clever woman understands these cultural mores and adjusts her strategy to the setting and situation.

Where you are, what you're doing, and at what time of day it is has a significant impact on the way men approach you and whether or not they approach you at all. The woman a man might approach at a house party might be the very same woman he's been talking himself out of meeting at the gym for the past two years.

Based on cultural expectations and social etiquette, there are just certain venues that make it easier for a man to give himself an excuse as to why he shouldn't pursue you. It's much easier to pursue a woman in a social setting where it's already culturally accepted that men and women are here to interact.

For instance, all types of men are likely to approach you at a social gathering where men and women are expected to meet and interact, like a house party, jazz café, and of course, your local tavern. On the other hand, if you've been working out at the same gym for the last two years and none of the strapping young men have taken the initiative to approach you, it's because men tend to think that women aren't open to being approached in this type of setting.

Because of this, I recommend a simple approach for women to consider following: The *less* culturally acceptable a place is for a woman to be approached by interested men the *more* initiative she might have to take to lower his risk of rejection and indicate interest. This isn't a hard and fast rule because you don't want to attract the attention of semi-interested men who only end up pursuing you because you "made it easy." But do keep in mind that you'll always have more of a challenge getting guys to pursue you in settings where men have been trained to avoid approaching women.

31

Consider lingering around the places you regularly visit, as it may open new

opportunities for you to meet interested men.

There might be a great guy right under your nose in a place you visit quite often. Why don't you ever see him? One reason is that you simply don't stick around long enough to give the poor guy a chance.

For example, a man won't hit on you in church. But he might attempt to get to know you after the service is done. Of course, if you bolt out the door and make a beeline straight for your car every Sunday, you're making it difficult for a potential suitor to try his hand.

Now, you might say to yourself that it's not your fault he hasn't built up enough courage to say something to you. But keep in mind that he has probably built up as much courage as he can muster to meet you – it's just that he's been waiting for an opportunity when you appear less "in a rush."

We live in a very busy culture where everyone always has something to do and somewhere to go. We thrive in a world where to look and feel busy gives us a sense of purpose and accomplishment. The only problem is, sometimes being in a rush can be a detriment to forming meaningful social interactions with people we don't know.

This may seem like common sense and it won't apply for all women, but *really* take the time to consider all the places you normally visit but *never* hang around longer than it takes you to accomplish your goal. Maybe you visit a local Starbucks quite often to pick up a latte but rarely stay, hang around, and even get to know the friendly baristas. Maybe you take an aerobics class but scram out of the door as soon as it's over instead of socializing with the other men and women.

Learn to stick around for a while and linger about the places you normally frequent and get to know people. Though you might not be approached by a man right away as you start doing this, eventually the men who do frequent such places will see you as being a warm, friendly woman who *enjoys meeting new people*.

So keep in mind that men aren't simpletons. They aren't going to try to get to know you if you look like someone who doesn't want to be known. Yes, a confident, mature man will go after what he wants no matter the situation. But this is the exception, not the rule. And as I've said before, if you want to place the odds in your favor you shouldn't rely on the exceptions.

I should note that while I do encourage sticking around to give interested guys a chance to meet you I do admit that this isn't an optimal strategy for certain venues. Take bars and clubs for instance. It usually behooves a woman to leave such places earlier than she would other social spots simply because the guys who only desire sexual conquest tend to make the majority of their moves much later.

From my past experience, I've seen bars and clubs fill up with men usually after 11:00 PM and have watched first hand how much more aggressive guys become with their pickup attempts since they've filled up on liquid courage (alcohol). Of course, this isn't a hard and fast rule since not *all* guys out late are going to be womanizers. But based on the law of averages, leaving such places early is a worthwhile strategy if you want to have a higher chance of avoiding being approached by men who only want to hook up. You've been warned.

32

A man will easily uncover a reason as to why a woman might be unapproachable. But by becoming *shieldless*, she strips away both his uncertainties and the lies he entertains in order to dissuade himself from pursuing. Thus the ardent admirer, if he fails to act boldly, will realize that it was not her that defeated him, but his own cowardice.

Make it extremely difficult for a man to live with himself if he doesn't approach you when he had the chance. How do you do this? You accomplish this by making it stupidly difficult for him to convince himself that "she's probably busy/difficult/seeing someone/etc." When you make being more approachable to men a priority, you'll realize that there are a number of things a woman can do to increase her openness to interesting social encounters by lowering a man's risk of rejection.

For instance, if you're wearing headphones and sunglasses, carrying a shopping bag, and speed walking through a busy mall, most interested guys have more than enough reasons to dissuade themselves that you're too much of a high-risk.

First there's the headphones which means he'd have to touch you, roadblock you, or wave his hands in an outlandish fashion like one of Jim Henson's Muppets in order to get your attention. Though fashionable, wearing sunglasses IN A MALL makes it difficult for a man to read your eyes – those very same eyes that work with your smile (or lack thereof) to let him know what his chances are. Your shopping bag tells him you're in the middle of something right now, and your speedy walk means his approach will look completely unnatural. So unnatural in fact that it will draw the attention of the people around him; people who might witness a mortifying public rejection.

You must consider what your first impressions are communicating to men everywhere you go only if making yourself more approachable is a priority. Some women might not be open to the effort involved, but I assume you aren't just reading this book for sheer entertainment.

33

Because it is rare for women to act with such audaciousness, a man's mind will race with insatiable curiosity should a woman be so bold as to offer the seat next to her.

This is a bold tactic that could yield rich rewards

for the courageous woman. If you see a man standing near you and there's an empty seat next to you, consider speaking up and offering it to him. This might be a "duh!" moment for the more confident woman, but keep in mind that not every female out there is willing or even aware enough of how her surroundings can work in her favor for meeting men.

A variation of this is if the guy you're interested in is far away from you. Once you've made eye contact with him at least once, if he looks in your direction again try smiling with him while motioning to the seat next to you. I'll admit that while this tactic isn't as subtle as the others, it is effective because of its directness. And keep in mind that quality guys especially appreciate a woman with forthrightness.

34

Men are very wary of women who appear to be the mini-celebrities of a particular venue. Unless he himself has a *higher* social status at that very location, the handsome observer will turn his eyes toward less intimidating women.

In certain social settings, if you appear to be extremely chummy with the local establishment it may dissuade a man from approaching you. This usually applies more to bars and nightclubs than it does other places. So even though in an earlier point (sticking around) I mentioned that getting to know people might improve your odds, being a mini-celebrity might not.

When a woman has a high social status in places like bars and nightclubs, to a relatively unknown guy, no matter what level his confidence, it tells him that she probably has the attitude of a mini-icon. Consider that if a guy is relatively unknown in a particular venue he'll feel much more comfortable connecting with a woman who's also relatively unknown. If you're known for hugging and giving cheek kisses to the regulars (and the staff), you give off that mini-icon vibe that might turn away a man who's more interested in connecting with a woman than having to prove himself worthy enough to even enter her spotlight.

Again, this isn't always the case but it's *much more common* for guys to pursue a woman whose social status is equal to or lesser than their own. It may seem ridiculous to a woman, but this is the nature of men.

Chapter 3

Change Your Attitude:
The Keys to Removing Your Invisible Anti-Guy Barrier

35

Know thyself. Be aware of the stumbling blocks towards courting male attention that are unique to you.

Hey, I get it. Some women don't want to "pursue" men for fear of being seen as desperate, needy, and/or easy. Some women would do more to be approachable but feel anxious and insecure around men they are attracted to. Both their limiting beliefs and anxiousness causes them to act less confidently around the men they're interested in, which then causes them to exhibit behaviors that either makes them *less* approachable or that do not indicate romantic interest.

Shyer girls may close themselves up and act weird around guys they find attractive while outgoing girls make themselves snappier to mask their insecurities. These sorts of behaviors can sometimes be huge stumbling blocks that cause some guys to sense discomfort or resistance in a woman as opposed to interest. Granted, this doesn't happen to all women and it might not be an issue for you. But if you find that guys quickly disappear soon after they show an interest in you, your problem may simply be in your behaviors.

Know which group you fall into because it will help you to fix the issue as you tactically implement any advice that helps you to be both more attractive and approachable to men.

36

You possess an attractive power beyond your comprehension. A woman's confidence intensifies all that is both beautiful and desirable about her. To a man, it makes her simply irresistible.

Confidence is the secret sauce to being more approachable to men or escalating a friendship into something more romantic. Surprised? You probably aren't, since it has become almost cliché advice by now that great guys love a confident woman. You probably know this already, but do you know why? Well, the reason great guys love confident women is because they make the courting process *so much more enjoyable*.

Imagine how utterly aggravating it must be for a guy who tries to make small talk with the cute girl at the gym and she basically closes up and gets all-weird on him. Although she gets weird because she's actually interested and therefore anxious, he actually has *no idea*. Her lack of confidence combined with his lack of experience creates a lost opportunity for two people who might have had something special.

A more experienced guy might see through her behavior and think it's cute and pursue her anyway. But men like this are the exception and, in some cases, a higher risk because *some* of the guys that fall into this group are fairly good at reading and seducing women…just for the fun of it. Think this is nonsense? Ask any guy if what I'm saying is even remotely true and he'll agree with me guaranteed. A confident woman is going to push past her insecurities in order to illustrate her interest *in a way men will understand*.

Being a confident woman isn't about being fearless or being extroverted. Because like I said in the introduction, an extroverted woman might show her anxiousness by being arrogant, edgy, or too difficult with a guy she finds attractive (even if she's not doing this purposefully this is how guys might perceive it). Being confident simply means that you recognize the risks involved in the courting process but you don't let those risks stop you from taking at least a little initiative to get what you want.

Yes, there's always a possibility that a guy might lose interest in you or even reject you outright, but it's par the course. But here's something else to consider: Most of the guys who are interested in you are far more anxious than you'll ever be. The risk of rejection and social embarrassment is very high and *very* real for men.

Because of this, men delight in those confident women who've learned how to send the right signals. You don't have to be aggressive in letting a guy know you're interested (most guys prefer to be the aggressor), but the right signal is the grease that oils the gears of romantic attraction. It speeds things up and makes the entire process much more fun and harmonious.

37

Contentment frees a woman from *needing*. When she is free from *needing*, she is free to engage with men with confidence and authenticity. When she is not desperate for the attention of men, a woman is more likely to receive it.

Have you ever noticed that you get *more* attention from men when you're already in a stable relationship? The same thing happens to men in that when they find themselves quite contented in a relationship, women who never knew they existed suddenly picked up their scent and became interested in them. This is a strange paradox that I'm sure has happened to you at some point if you've ever been in a fun and stable relationship. But why does this happen?

Well, one reason is because when you're in an enjoyable relationship you may find yourself simply being yourself around the opposite sex. Because you're not trying to impress a guy to get his attention, you're free to let your inner feminine charms radiate.

When you're not under any pressure to attract a guy you might find yourself interacting with men with much more confidence. An introvert would no longer close up or get "weird" around attractive men and an extrovert would no longer seem so difficult or testy.

Both types of women can simply engage with men with no attachment to the outcomes, which then frees them from the nervous energy that would have kept interested men at bay.

So how does a woman act like she's already in a relationship? Simple. Have no attachments to the outcome when you interact with men. It's a mental attitude that will take time to fully embrace, but the rewards are worth it. When you don't *need* a certain guy to like you, you'll quickly realize that you have nothing to fear. Be free from the outcome (landing a boyfriend) and simply enjoy interacting with men for its own sake. Sometimes having no goal is the best way to getting what you really want.

38

If she feels inclined to do so, it is quite acceptable for a woman to initiate contact with her Mr. McDreamy. However, this behavior is only encouraged if the woman in question has learned how to separate the good men from the womanizers.

If you feel inclined to approach a man you're interested in, do so. If you've been struggling with the idea that a man might think of you as promiscuous if you initiate contact with him, I'm here to tell you that this couldn't be further from the truth.

A man will respond to a woman based on who he is to the core. If he's a player he will respond like a player and yes, he will see you as an easy target. On the other hand, if he's a good guy who feels flattered by your approach, he'll see you as a woman who knows what she wants and, if he's interested as well, will reciprocate in kind. A guy with a good heart is going to see you as being fun, sociable, and confident which are all attractive qualities in a woman.

While I don't advocate *chasing* or *pursuing* a man, there's nothing wrong with initiating contact. Once you've initiated contact however, you <u>must</u> let him lead. Here's where things get tricky, because if he doesn't "bite your bait" so to speak, and pursue you, then he's just not *that* interested.

If you're going to initiate contact then you must be willing to handle the fact that some men might want to continue seeing you so long as you continue to take the initiative. Don't waste time on guys like this. If you work up the courage to initiate contact with a guy in some way and he doesn't *take the lead* from there, cut your losses and move on. You want a man who is proactive about getting what he wants, especially when it comes to a relationship with a woman.

39

Whether by behavior or appearance, no woman is above the duty of improving her attractiveness to the type of man she desires.

If you think you're "above" having to fine-tune your level of attractiveness in order to get a boyfriend, you, my dear, are delusional. Just as no man is "above" the arduous task of becoming an attractive man of high character in order to become a homing beacon for a great girlfriend no woman is "above" the grueling personal development that's necessary to attract higher quality men.

Being willing to work on being more approachable while getting out of your comfort zone is half the battle. Don't fall into the false notion that working on your attractiveness makes you shallow. Your feminine beauty and social warmth can be fine-tuned in such a way that the right guy can become helplessly captivated by you. Don't sell yourself short by ignoring this aspect of your personal growth.

40

Act the part of a woman who has too much love to give. Great guys have zero interest in women who take more than they give. Instead, be generous with your warmth.

A simple shift in your attitude will make a big difference in how you go about interacting with men in social settings. Begin to see yourself as a woman who has way more to offer others than what you take from them. An abundance attitude leads to generous behavior that makes a woman appear magnanimous and a pleasure to be around.

She's not out to get men to buy her drinks and she's not concerned with trying to avoid unwanted attention either. She's merely focused on sharing her warmth with others and making them feel better about themselves for spending time with her. So while your intention is to meet a great guy somewhere as you venture out, your focus is on making every interaction you have with another human being a generous one.

41

If she wishes to avoid wasting her energies, a woman would be wise to spend the majority of her social outings at venues where good, compatible men are more likely to congregate.

If you want to catch saltwater fish you don't buy a rifle and head to the nearest forest. If you want to hunt moose, planning a hunting trip to The Bahamas is going to be a complete waste of your time. The same applies for attracting the attention of a *high-quality* man. Go where the game is! No, better yet…go where the *best* game is!

If you want to attract the attention of men in which you're more likely to have a high level of compatibility, spend the majority of your time in environments where they're most likely to be. If you attempt to use the tips in this book only in places like bars and clubs you're likely to attract more *unwanted* attention from men. One reason for this is that men with shorter-term dating goals who have refined their ability to create near instant chemistry with women frequent such places.

The other reason is that women with short-term dating goals also frequent such places as well, which therefore attracts the attention of all kinds of men in general. Because women like this may be more confident in approaching and interacting with men, it will make it more difficult for a woman with a less assertive approach towards attracting a man's attention. In short, bars and clubs are not the ideal places for meeting relationship-minded guys.

I say all this to bring home the point that if you're most interested in attracting the attention of a man who wants a long-term relationship, you must consistently place yourself in environments that attract men who are *more likely* to share your values. This is perhaps the most important thing to consider as you implement the advice in this book because it will make filtering out the men who approach you a lot easier. You're also less likely to experience any unwanted surprises when you do begin dating a man.

Once again, do yourself a favor by improving your odds. Go where the good men are, the relationship-minded, masculine guys with a strong moral framework. Happy hunting!

42

The identity you've chosen or settled for is not set in stone. Who "you" are is really a fluid concept.

Admittedly, I got this from the movie, *Hitch*, but it was such a great moment in the movie that reflects the idea behind "changing your attitude" that I decided to add it here. *Hitch* stars Will Smith as a dating coach called, Hitch, who helps guys woo their true love. During the part where a guy Hitch was helping didn't think that the shoes Hitch was making him wear on a date were "him", Hitch replied that it was "him" who bought the shoes and that it was "him" who now looks good in them. Hitch was implying that "him" (the identity the guy accepted as himself) was a fluid concept that could adapt and change positively to achieve his goal.

Nowadays, whenever I hear someone say, "Well, that's just not really *me*" what I really hear is "I'm comfortable with my choices and I don't really feel the need to try something else." Much of the advice in this book focuses on adjusting your behavior on a consistent basis so that you can attract the attention of potentially great guys. But I know for a fact that some women will read the advice and say to themselves, "Well, that's just not really *me*" meaning that they're *more* comfortable with who they are than they are *determined* to get the results they want.

Yes, you can be yourself and attract a great guy, but like Hitch said in the movie, "you" is a fluid concept. "You" can change your body language to be more attractive to men. "You" can change the way you think so that asking your crush out for coffee won't seem like something outlandish for you. "You" are an ever-changing, ever-growing individual. And as long as something doesn't cross your moral boundaries, "you" should be open to changing how you relate with men if you want to have more success in your love life.

43

All male attention is not created equal. The more a woman caters to the male's sexual desires, the lower the quality in manly attention she will attract. A man's imagination is primed by visual hints of promiscuity, but his curiosity is primed by female modesty. Therefore, if she wishes to effectively filter the cads from the gentlemen, a woman would be wise to exercise modesty in both her dress and behavior.

For relationship-minded men, modesty equates to quality. If you're interested in men who want more than just a one-night stand or who don't intend on wasting your valuable, youthful years, female modesty is one of those qualities that can make high-quality men take notice of you.

Exercising modesty means that a woman dresses and behaves in a way that makes her feminine beauty all the more sacred and worth unraveling. With the biggest benefit being that a modest woman gains the attention of men who are more likely to *respect* her. Men speak the language of respect when it comes to relationships. Therefore, a man gives his love to a woman only *after* she has gained his respect.

For example, you can dress so irresistibly to a man that he cannot help but adore and venerate you, or you can sex things up to the point where all he wants to do is throw you in bed. If you dress and behave in a way merely to be craved and desired by men, you'll have a much harder time filtering out the good ones from the slime when they initiate contact with you.

Modesty in both dress and behavior separates you first off because it communicates to a man that you firmly believe that you have more to offer men than just your looks. I saved this point for last in this section because when you're out with your girlfriends or even surrounded by other women, you want to make yourself highly approachable to men…but the *right* kind of men.

Men know that women want their attention. The attention of men feeds a woman's instinctual desire to *be desired* by *desirable (high status) men*, which is natural. However, modesty communicates to a man that a woman's sole priority is *not* the attention of men, meaning she's risen above this sort of thing. So while you want to make yourself more approachable, exercising modesty will keep you from going overboard just to get a man's attention as well as make you even more attractive to higher quality men who actively search for this attribute in a woman.

I know all this sounds counterintuitive, but this is how men think. When a man first meets you he knows absolutely nothing about you. Therefore, because the human mind can only make meaning or ascribe value to something, he must both *define* and *evaluate* you on his first impressions. Modesty is the one quality that tells a man that you have other interests in life than attracting men. It also tells him that if he were to pursue you he would never have to question your loyalty to him since you're not the kind of woman who craves male attention.

So while a hot and extremely sexually provocative dressed woman may garner *a ton* of male attention from both good guys and players, the good guys aren't going to go out of their way to pursue her for a relationship. It's the ugly truth. And believe me, I've seen guys time and time again lose interest in, break up with, or simply ignore even very attractive women due to appearance and behavioral issues involving modesty.

Chapter 4

Reel Him In:
Simple Tips for Being Irresistible and Securing His Interest

44

More often than not, a woman may overlook the subtle signs of male curiosity if the handsome observer masks his interest in flirtatious behavior. Watch for those subtle and not-so-subtle signs of flirting that men exhibit when they're interested in a woman.

Things like playful banter, flattery, light touching, prolonged eye contact, and qualifying (where a man tries to assess your level of interest by how much you want his approval) are a few examples of ways a man may flirt with you. Knowing the signs of male flirting behavior will give you an edge where you'll be able to pick up on a man's level of interest by the intensity of his flirtatiousness. And once you're able to pick up on his level of interest you can better judge whether or not it's worth engaging in his courting game.

Women who are less informed about dealing with men cannot tell when a man is flirting with them. Because of low self-esteem or simply due to a lack of experience, they may think that a man is just being "nice" instead of seeing his behavior for what it really is – an attempt to create sexual tension. Learn the many ways men attempt to create chemistry with a woman so that you won't miss any opportunities to reel in a potential admirer.

45

Face your bold pursuer, looking directly into his eyes during the conversation. Do not stare audaciously, but rather regard him with attentive smiles.

If a man approaches you, he thinks you're beautiful. Regardless of his intentions, this in and of itself is a compliment to *you*. If an interested guy is trying to communicate with you don't insult him by looking away, staring at your smartphone, or turning your body away from him. Give him your undivided attention and really try to live in the moment by facing and focusing on him. While this may seem like common sense to some women (the ones with even a reasonable amount of etiquette), others may overlook this aspect of their behavior.

High-quality men, because of the high level of respect they have for others tend to expect at least some level of respect to be reciprocated to them. A woman might quickly lose the interest of a man who approaches her simply by failing to be respectful with her body language. Facing a man tells him that you're open to his advances and that you enjoy his company. Not facing him obviously does just the opposite.

46

Submissive body language is very attractive to a man in search of a loving and loyal girlfriend. In close quarters, as you communicate with a man, ensure that you do not remain on higher ground.

This is a very subtle tactic that every woman looking to garner the favor of high-quality men should keep in her seduction arsenal. If your surroundings can allow it, ensure that your eye level is equal to or *lower* than the man you're interacting with. For example, if he's sitting down and you're standing, as quickly and as effortlessly as you can, get on equal eye level with him by sitting next to or across from him.

Reeling in a high-quality man means that you must cater to his masculine identity. And one very important aspect of that identity is his need to feel high status (and thereby highly desirable) by the opposite sex. Taking a seat next to him or sitting low as he stands, etc., relays the subconscious message that you consider him a high status male and therefore highly desirable. Submissive body language like this moves pass his conscious mind and connects with his subconscious ideals of being adored by a beautiful woman.

47

The woman who wears an intoxicating fragrance will not easily be forgotten. Her very presence will linger with a man and his mind will remain seized by her enchantments. Such a woman will have little trouble reeling in a handsome stranger or even an interested acquaintance.

I honestly believe that the power of scent is highly underestimated when it comes to attracting the attention of men. Yes, men are highly visual in nature and can easily become captivated by a single glance of a woman. But when a woman has also taken the time and effort necessary to make her scent irresistible, she also becomes absolutely unforgettable. To this day, I can still remember some of the instances in which I've come across women whose scents were enchanting.

If a man approaches you, he already thinks you're beautiful, but if your signature scent is alluring enough he won't be able to help himself. You would have already conquered two of his physical senses, which is more than enough for a man to wade through hell and high water just to get and *keep* your attention.

If you have guy friends you trust, test out various perfumes and body oils and get their honest opinions. Don't trust your girlfriends on this. The scent that your girlfriend may love probably won't be the same one that quickens a man's pulse.

48

Men crave the sincere admiration of women. Thus, a genuine, well-crafted compliment will stir a man's confidence and make him feel *manlier* in your presence. No man can resist or soon forget a woman who makes him like himself even more.

Flattery might not get you very far, but sincere compliments might, especially when dealing with men. If there's something you genuinely admire about your admirer, let him know. You might falsely believe that complimenting a man you've just met might give him the impression that you're helplessly drawn to him. It's true that you don't want to come off as seeming completely enamored by Mr. Tall-Dark-and-Handsome but you can still pay him a genuine compliment.

If he says something funny, after you laugh and/or giggle, tell him you think he's "funny" or "hilarious." If he offered you his seat before striking up a conversation with you, tell him that you think he's quite the rare gentleman. If there's something about his style of clothing (or accessories) that you like, point it out.

The potency of the compliment will depend on the

guy. Complimenting whatever he values most or has placed a lot of effort in developing is going to really get his attention. Men who enjoy sharing their knowledge (yes, that's me) love being complimented on their wisdom, breadth/depth of understanding, or having helped someone learn something useful. If your Mr. McDreamy appears to have the body of the Greek god Adonis, then it's quite clear that he pays special attention to his physique.

Now, if you really want to make him feel special, compliment something about his character or behavior. High-quality men also pay close attention to the development of their character, which means he might appreciate a compliment that highlights any one of his virtues. The point is to be sincere with your praise but also make him feel special in your presence. Men crave the sincere admiration of women. Remember that.

49

If you have enjoyed your first interaction with your perfect gentleman, ensure that he is firmly aware of it. Cast your fears aside and indicate your hopes of a future meeting between you both. Once you have hinted...let him lead.

Meeting a woman somewhere random, having an engaging interaction with her, and then hearing her say,

"Hey, this was fun. We should do it again sometime" with a warm, genuine smile on her face is *rare*, even for the most seasoned Casanova. Women who might be less outgoing might think that it's rude to imply any kind of interest in a man, but this is a ridiculous notion. If you feel a connection with Mr. McDreamy, close the sale. Say something genuine and positive about the interaction, and then *hint* to him that you'd like to see him again, perhaps even soon.

Remember…be *mature*. If he didn't feel the same way and he rejects you, it's okay. It won't kill you, I promise. Fortune favors the bold! So don't be afraid to let a man know that you've genuinely enjoyed his company and would like to do so in the future.

Chapter 5

Love At First Sight:
How to Captivate Him With a Flawless First Impression

50

The first thing the ardent admirer notices in a woman is her physical beauty. Her bodily features, her style of dress, and her grooming will be quickly appraised. They will thus determine whether or not he considers her merely commonplace or a precious jewel among mediocre women.

Here's the blunt truth: Eighty to ninety percent of your chances of being approached by a man is dependent on how physically attractive you are *to him*. This may turn some women off, but this is the reality. Unless he's already a friend of yours and he's attracted to both your appearance and personality, for a total stranger, the only thing a man has to evaluate his interest in you is primarily your appearance and then after watching you for awhile, your behavior.

This is a good thing because a woman's physical appearance is very much in her control. When you really think about, it's even more manageable than her personality or even character. While personality traits and character traits take time and effort to develop, a woman can literally make herself even slightly more attractive to men almost overnight if she knows how to accentuate her best features.

When a man first lays eyes on you, on a

subconscious level, he decides whether or not he's attracted to your facial structure and your body type. If a guy decides he likes a facial structure and body type far different from yours, there's nothing you can do about this, and that's fine. Such things are completely out of your control.

However, the things that are at least somewhat in your control include things like: weight and fitness, makeup, hairstyle, clothing, body hair, and even posture; all things that men notice in a split second when they look at you. These first impressions of your physical beauty make lasting impressions on a guy. This is how nature designed us. Having a beautiful woman to show off to the world is proof of our ability to attract a highly desirable mate. This is why your physical appearance is super important to a man, because on some level, being with an attractive woman makes us feel better about ourselves.

Consider that aside from improving your chances of having guys approach you, one of the other benefits of putting a lot of thought into your looks is that it will separate the boys from the men. Self-assured men will see a gorgeous woman and think, *"Wow, where has she been all my life? She's exactly what I've been searching for!"* While a less self-assured man will look at a gorgeous woman and think, *"Wow! I can't believe how gorgeous she is. She's definitely out of my league. She probably won't want to talk to me."* Looking great places you on the radar of more ambitious men – those who want the best in life.

I cannot stress how important it is for you to <u>learn</u> what <u>men</u> find attractive. What you and your girlfriends think is a cute outfit might rate as 'meh!' on most men's attractiveness scale. I'm also not going to waste your time and tell you that men just want you to "be yourself" when it comes to physical appearance. No. Unless "being yourself" means that you're already working on increasing your confidence and self-esteem by improving your physical beauty, it's bad advice. The clichéd "be yourself" advice works best when it comes to radiating your personality and staying true to your beliefs and values. But in all honesty, the advice is almost useless in regards to physical appearance.

Also, don't use the excuse of a woman's character being way more important than her looks. While it IS true that a woman's character is way more important than her looks, no guy is going to give you a chance if you *neglect* to take care of your physical appearance. And in any case, such *neglect* for appreciating what God gave you does, in fact, reflect your character.

So keep in mind that until a man gets to know the real you, to him, at least at first glance…you are your appearance.

51

The woman who wishes to be a rarity among others must appeal to the masculine subconscious. The more distinctive her dress and manner appears when compared to that of a man's the more she will stand out. If she

wishes to captivate a truly masculine man she must be unapologetically feminine.

This bit of wisdom is an offshoot of the previous one because I'd like to stress a point that some women tend to overlook with their physical appearance. If you're interested in attracting the attention of more mature (not necessarily older), masculine men, be as feminine as you possibly can in dress and manner.

Because opposites attract each other, men who revel in the fact that they are men adore women who embrace their femininity. And the only way he's going to know straight off the bat if you're the kind of woman who embraces her femininity is through your physical appearance and behavior.

This sort of topic would require a book of its own, but think of it this way. Anything that makes you look, feel, and behave as *different* from a man as humanly possibly can be considered feminine. For instance, it is culturally acceptable for a woman to wear either pants or a dress. It is not so for men. Men cannot and do not wear dresses (except for weirdoes). Therefore, a pretty summer dress, at least to most red-blooded men, is *way* more attractive than a pair of khakis.

And though chided for it in today's post-feminist world, statistically, men *still* find long hair *more* attractive than short hair. Long hair makes a woman look different from a man, and as I've already mentioned, different is good for attraction. Think about it. If even just a little bit more facial hair on a guy can make him appear more attractive to you, think about how men respond to changes in your appearance that bring out your femininity.

52

A woman's eyes are her greatest assets for safely communicating her interest to a man. A coquettish glance with a demure smile can quickly embolden your handsome observer's confidence to pursue you. Learn how to use your eyes to your advantage.

Eye contact is the single most effective way for encouraging a man to approach you. It's not as passive a tactic as smiling and therefore you, as a woman, take on a bit more risk. The big benefit of eye contact however, is that it is a clear and <u>direct</u> indication that a woman is, at least, curious about a man and, depending on the nature of the eye contact, wants him to do something about her curiosity.

If you make eye contact with a guy, it first states that you like what you see. If you make eye contact with a guy and linger, even if just for a moment, if states that you like what you see and you'd like for him to come over. The former (a more modest tactic) inspires a man's curiosity in you while the latter inspires both his curiosity and boosts his confidence in wooing you.

More confident men won't need a lingering look, while less confident men might require one. My personal opinion is that the use of the lingering look should be situational. For example, unless you're interested in attracting the attention of men who only want to hook up with you, I would suggest refraining from using the lingering look in places where such men actively hunt (i.e., bars and clubs).

On the other hand, if there's an acquaintance that you've had your eye on for a while now and the chemistry between you is a sure thing, a lingering look might be just what he needs to finally ask you out. So as you can see, depending on the kind of attention you want to attract, the level of your flirtatious eye contact should vary based on place and situation.

Whether or not you linger with your look, you want to ensure that you smile at some point in your eye contact so that the interaction seems *intentional* on some level. Sure, you can be more demure with your eye contact by quickly looking away when he glances in your direction, but failing to smile invitingly before doing so will only waste the opportunity. If you use the demure, coy-like approach by shifting your eyes away from him right after he looks at you, you must ensure that you smile with him first before glancing off in another direction (I explain the reason why in the next point).

Now, you may be wondering how much eye contact is necessary for a man to get the message. It will depend on the guy in question, but I suggest that your eye contact with any one guy should add up to anywhere between five to ten seconds depending on the situation. Now, when I say five to ten seconds I mean the amount of time you spend *in total* trading eye contact with any one man in any given setting should add up to this amount. You can shoot him a quick one-second flirty glance or even hold an attentive three-second look. But you want to use your glances at various intervals rather than get into a five to ten second staring contest. Don't get into a staring contest…that's just creepy. Any guy who, after trading looks with a woman for five to ten seconds collectively, doesn't initiate contact with you is not worth knowing.

I don't encourage women to waste their time on man-boys who don't have the gall to take a hint and take action to get what they want. Remember, you want to attract men who both know what they want and who go after what they want. Don't waste your captivating gazes on wussies.

53

There are two ways a woman can make a man blind to the other women around her. First, she must dress and groom better than the women she most associates with. And secondly, she must dress and groom at least slightly better than the venue requires. *Exceptionality* is the fair price she must pay for a man's *undivided* attention.

Men love it when a woman takes the time and energy to look good *in spite of* the generally accepted decorum of dress for a particular environment. Put another way, men really do notice it when a woman goes out of her way to be stunning, no matter the setting.

Again, dressing beyond the basic requirements of your environment, even by a little, places the odds in your favor because it makes you stand out amongst your peers. And if you didn't realize it by now, here's the ugly truth: You are competing with other women.

Of course, you don't have to wear a bunch of makeup every single time you leave the house, but do consider that even just a little makeup goes a long way to keep you from blending in with other women. A pretty summer dress, pinned up hair, and just a dab of makeup could net you the attention of an attractive stranger during a casual trip to the bank or supermarket. In fact, this might be the very same handsome stranger that might have overlooked you (since you would have blended in with the other frumpily dressed women) had you decided to don your favorite sweatpants and T-shirt instead. You know which ones I'm referring to.

I've known young women with natural beauty, exotic even, that would make most females turn goblin green with envy, but for some reason they always seemed to do just the bare minimum to look good. On the other hand, I've known some women whose natural beauty were pretty basic (by my tastes at least) but who were still immensely attractive due to their habit of dressing well, even when the occasion didn't call for it.

Dressing well, even when you don't have to, speaks volumes about your character (there's that word again) and the value you place on yourself. It's not shallow for a woman to go out of her way to look great as often as she can. Of course, as with everything one must exercise some sort of balance. You can look great in the supermarket, bank, or even during a trip to the dentist, but just don't go overboard with it. While a man may find you stunningly beautiful if you're dressed to impress while waiting on line at the DMV, you might look just a bit ridiculous to him if you look as if you're going to the club while running the treadmill at Bally's.

54

In the eyes of your perfect gentleman, the most encouraging smile is an effortless and inviting one. To him, a woman's smile must be perceived as intentional if she wishes to lure him to approach her.

This should be common sense to all women so I'm not going to tell you to do it. I AM, however, going to say a few words about the *nature* of your smile and why it makes a huge difference.

Now, when the man in your sights catches you looking at him you should, of course, send him a warm, inviting smile. But don't call me Captain Obvious just yet because what you may think is an *inviting* smile to a man it could be seen as something a bit more vague. The level of warmth and invitingness in your smile will depend on just how natural your smile actually is.

If you make eye contact with your Mr. McDreamy and, being nervous, you shoot him a quick and evasive smile it will look to him as if you were accidently looking in his direction when he looked at you. Your smile won't be received as warm and inviting, instead he'll think that you didn't <u>intend</u> to look in his direction and you just smiled to be nice. Notice the key word in that last sentence? It was "intend." Your smile, no matter how quick or subtle, needs to have an intention.

On the other hand, you don't want your smile to make him think that you're on the brink of losing your mind. If a guy glances at you and you decide to ramp up your smile by grinning like the Cheshire Cat, don't be surprised if he quickly looks away and darts for the nearest exit. Some women, in an attempt to make themselves more approachable, make their smiles appear very unnatural. Unless he has a weird man-crush on The Joker, an unnatural grin isn't going to reel him in.

If smiling at a guy feels forced, it's definitely going to look awkward. If smiling at a man makes you uncomfortable (because you're anxious), it's going to look awkward as well. Only you can judge whether or not you're a warm-grinner, a cute-smirker, or a demure-beamer. Use what works most naturally for you, but don't be afraid of trying something new if what you've been doing hasn't been working.

So should you decide to work on perfecting your smile to make it more *inviting*, keep in mind that you *will*, at times, find yourself smiling awkwardly. Practice makes perfect, so don't be afraid or feel ashamed to practice smiling at men, even if you have to look ridiculous in the process.

It's also important for a woman to consider the

smile she wears when her face is at rest. As I keep repeating throughout this book, men are observing your behavior and often spot you long before you see them. Walking around with the "too-cool-to-smile" diva look on your face is uninviting and not warm at all.

The same goes for a sourpuss face that screams misery and cantankerousness. Most men will want to avoid women who wear such faces, save for the pick-up artist types who might enjoy this sort of challenge. Be warm, open, fun, and friendly. In other words, let your smile be *inviting*.

Smiling is perhaps the easiest thing a woman can do to indicate her interest in a man while lowering his risk of rejection. It is the most passive, risk averse strategy a woman can utilize towards encouraging men to take a chance on meeting her.

To a man, the smile of a woman is a timeless and obvious sign that she's either interested or in the least, not repulsed by the man in her sights. And when used in tandem with eye contact, it might be all a woman needs in her arsenal to pique the curiosity of an ardent admirer.

Chapter 6

How Men Think:
Understanding the Mind of an Interested Man

55

As a woman develops into a more attractive and thusly, approachable individual, she will undoubtedly garner the attention of both relationship-minded men and Lotharios. However, she can gain much clarity of a man's true intentions so long as she appeals to his longing to both give and receive respect.

You may find that as your "fishing techniques" improve you may also increase the amount of poisonous fish in your net as well. The challenge then is to be able to quickly figure out a man's true intentions and filter out the good ones from the toxic ones. But how does a woman become more approachable while keeping the toxic guys out of her net as much as possible? Simple, by catering to a man's deepest desires.

There's one thing that all men need and want from a woman they're interested in having a relationship with. Yes, we all know that men want sex and will say and do just about anything on the path for sexual conquest. But there's another need, an even deeper need, which compels a man to pursue and court a woman for the long-term. It's the need for respect.

A man needs to feel respected by a woman before

he can *allow* himself to fall in love with her. On the other hand, a man needs to feel respect *for* a woman before he can commit to her. Read those last two sentences several more times and internalize them because they are, essentially, the secret to understanding men.

Sexual desire is *not* a good measure of a man's interest in you and the more you cater to this particular primal drive the more difficulty you'll have in assessing both his character and his motives. But by acting respectfully towards a man you make it easy for him to be authentic with you, which will show you his true colors.

Once a man feels that he can be himself around you, he will quickly reveal his intentions, which, in the case of Mr. Wrong, will show itself through his sexual aggressiveness (overtly-sexual flirting, suggesting you come to his place, etc.). Being very respectful towards men works wonders because it quickly connects you to authentic guys who see you as a long-term pursuit while revealing the time-wasters who only want sex.

Giving a man respect triggers something in the masculine subconscious that piques his curiosity, maintains his interest, intensifies his attraction, and solidifies his trust. When a man trusts you, he will open up himself to you *much* more quickly which will reveal everything you need to know about what he wants from you.

Courting a man's respect is the single most effective way for figuring out if he's interested in a relationship or just sex. Men may pursue a woman to the ends of the earth for sex, but once that need is satisfied, they move on in search of more *sexual variety*.

Respect on the other hand, when both courted and given to a man, fills a deeper void, one that cannot be easily satisfied during a one-night-stand. A man knows that in order to earn a woman's respect he must *act* in an admirable way…consistently. He must show himself as both a good man and a man who's good at being a man. If a woman's character (attitudes and behavior) *demands* respect, her value skyrockets in the eyes of a high-quality man. And as is human nature, we fall in love with that which we value highly.

Train yourself to cater to the masculine desire to give and receive respect. This has everything to do from the way you dress to the way you communicate with a man. Some women are drop dead gorgeous but remain perpetually single because they have no idea how to court a man's respect nor do they know how to give it unconditionally in a loving relationship. Men of high character can tell very quickly whether or not a woman has more substance than style, and most won't waste their time or resources on a woman who struggles to be respectful.

If a man seduces you and attains the sex he so desires without paying a price first, there's a greater chance for him bailing on you the minute you demand more of him (which you always will). Cater to a man's appeal for respect and you'll find it exceptionally easy to filter out the good guys from the slime.

A man only interested in sex won't put in the effort needed to win your heart since respect must be earned. You will earn his affection by giving him respect and you will increase his level of commitments by courting his respect. You, as a woman, are the gatekeeper to sexual pleasure; always remember that.

56

Sometimes a woman's extraordinary beauty or social standing may result in her loneliness. If the men you regularly meet deem you as out-of-their-league or higher class, they will be twice as frightened to approach you. Their worship of your beauty or popularity is their downfall.

Men are simple but strange creatures. The more attractive a man thinks you are the less chances he might think he has with you and therefore, the more he won't want to mess things up. In other words, sometimes a man with high levels of interest in you will be twice as likely *not* to approach you due to this paralyzing fear.

The woman that will usually have this problem is either extremely attractive (models, exotic-looking women, etc.) or very much intimidating (out-of-his-league, higher class, etc.) to the guys she normally comes across on a regular basis.

The fear of "messing things up" with an attractive woman paralyzes a lot of guys so that they fail to take any action. It's almost as if they convince themselves that since their chances of failing with this one-of-a-kind woman is so high they might as not even try. Men like this haven't matured to the point of being pro-risk in order to get what they want.

You cannot do anything about situations like this because you'll have no idea he's interested if he's so afraid to mess things up. By implementing the advice in this book you *may* be able to coax him into doing something about his interest, but the ball will still predominately be in his court.

57

For an interested man, the potential benefits of approaching a woman must always outweigh the risks. Therefore the question a woman must honestly ask herself is: Am I worth the risk?

Most guys do whatever they can to minimize the risk of rejection when it comes to the opposite sex. These risks include emotional pain, public embarrassment, exposed insecurities, rudeness, a wounded ego, a drink to the face, ridicule by your girlfriends, ridicule by his friends, ridicule by *other* girls you don't know but who witnessed the rejection, etc., etc.

For a lot of guys these risks *seem* very real, which

means that the *potential benefits* of approaching a woman must always outweigh the risks. Read that last line again because it is the quintessential, singular thought process of all single men when they see an attractive woman. For a man to approach you, introduce himself, and engage you he must have already decided, even if done subconsciously, that he'd rather face the risk of rejection than let this opportunity pass. The problem with most guys is that they allow their fear of rejection to override their desire for female companionship.

It's only when a man matures enough in his worldly experiences does he learn to enjoy the risks associated with pursuing the fairer sex. Either that or a man has to be so smitten by what he sees that his desire overcomes his "better judgment." This is why your only two jobs as a single woman is:

1. Make yourself as attractive as you can so that a man ends up hating himself for not approaching you (it happens to ALL men, trust me), and…

2. Make yourself more approachable more often so as to increase the odds of interested men going out of their way to pursue you.

I mention all this to stress the point that you should always be at least somewhat aware of whether or not you're lowering the risk or rejection or increasing it. You can't do anything about the level of confidence a man has in himself but you can control just how open, warm, and approachable you make yourself. You can make rejection easy for him (as is the point of this book) or difficult. But to assess just how easy (or difficult) you're making it for guys you need to understand how single men think when they're hoping to meet someone special.

58

Empathizing with men can help to lower your inhibitions and neurosis, leading you to enjoy more authentic interactions with potential suitors.

If you were a guy and you saw an attractive woman at a social gathering, how would you approach her? From now on, whenever you do go out with the hopes of interacting with the opposite sex consciously try to see things from a man's point of view. Put yourself in his shoes and consider what a guy might be going through at any given moment where there are attractive women that he might like to meet. The benefit of this habit is that it takes you out of your own head so that you're not so focused on your own behaviors.

When you're not so self-conscious two things happen. First, you allow yourself to act naturally around the opposite sex, which means you'll enjoy more authentic and higher quality interactions with men. Secondly, since you're focusing on the men in the room you're more likely to *empathize* with what they're dealing with.

A few astute gentlemen will pick up your empathic vibe *very* quickly and they'll see you as a low risk, high reward pursuit. Being empathic gives you insight into how others are feeling. And when you sense that the handsome, calm, and confident-looking man across the room has his own insecurities towards meeting a stunning woman like yourself you're likely to feel a sudden boost of confidence that might prompt you to make a little lingering eye contact with him.

59

Be reticent with your signals when interacting with what appears to be a highly dominant man. The more signals you send him the more he'll assume you want him. If a man is assured that a woman desires him more than he does her, the game is lost for her.

For shyer men, the more attractive he thinks you are the more signals you might need to send him. For a more confident man who believes that he deserves to date an attractive woman like you, the fewer signals you should send him because he's already aware of his high-status. Every man has a sliding scale in his mind in regards to how beautiful a woman is and the kind of attention he believes he deserves from her.

This isn't something you can change, but the more you interact with men and learn their behavior the better you'll get at judging just how much signals a certain kind of guy might require before you give up on him altogether. The more dominant the guy the less signals you'll want to send since to him it will mean that he has *less* work to do to woo you.

60

Expect to receive less attention from men at certain venues and even at certain times of the day. The less culturally acceptable a setting is for courtship interaction between the opposite sexes, the less likely it is for you to be approached by men.

This may be common sense but I decided to add it in anyway. Some men, most men, will *not* approach a woman at certain venues. Also, even if a man doesn't mind approaching women in a wide variety of situations, his *reasons* for approaching might not always be the same.

Let me explain.

The same guy that might approach you in a bar might be petrified to even say "Hello" to you at the gym. He may believe that meeting women at a bar is more natural and therefore women expect to be approached. On the other hand, he may think that women don't want to be approached at the gym since many of them walk-around looking all busy and focused (with headphones on) on their workouts. Even a pickup artist who specializes in "nighttime game" might shy away from approaching women in the light of day due to the higher risks of rejection (and lower chances of sexual conquest with slightly inebriated women).

So what's the moral of the story? It's not as simple as categorizing some men as "shy" and some as "confident." Different men will be bolder in meeting a woman depending on the venue, time of day, and what they expect to gain from the interaction.

61

Your shyness or outgoingness will not hinder a man from showing an interest in you so long as you're willing to send him a signal he can recognize. If your comfort zone has become a hindrance to meeting Mr. Right, expand it. Fortune favors the bold!

I've flirted with and dated both shy and outgoing women. The interesting thing is that the better I got with the opposite sex the easier it was for me to tell when both shy girls and outgoing girls were interested in me. With that knowledge I was much more successful in meeting and dating some pretty phenomenal girls, all up until I found the one that I wanted to spend my life with.

The take away here is that shy girls don't have to worry about becoming Miss Personality just to get a guy's attention and outgoing girls don't have to worry about toning their personalities down to the point of becoming bland and boring just to get a guy. For example, most of the girls that I preferred getting to know were more shy and reserved in nature. That was my preference simply because I enjoy being the dominant aggressor in the game of attraction.

But admittedly, not all guys are like me, and that's perfectly fine. A friend of mine is far more laid back than I am and it's clear that his wife was the bolder one during the initial stages of their courtship. She came, she saw, she conquered, and he didn't find it off-putting that she was so forthcoming with her interests. Different guys prefer and pursue different kinds of women. And this is why it's so important to stay true to who you are as you interact with men.

If you're an outgoing girl, simply train yourself to indicate your interest in the language men understand. Tone it down if the guys you're attracted to often perceive you as "difficult" or "testy." If you're a shy girl, ramp things up a bit by showing more signs of interest. It may be awkward and stressful for you at first, but if you want to have more opportunities to *choose* a worthy suitor...relax and just send him a signal. The man who wants you bad enough will take it from there. Guaranteed.

About Bruce Bryans

Bruce Bryans is a successful author who has written numerous best-selling books for men and women who want to improve the quality of their relationships. After writing for various online publications on the topics of dating and relationships, he ran a successful romance advice website where his insightful articles and newsletters helped improve people's love lives one-by-one.

Years later, Bruce decided to focus his time and efforts on writing and publishing books with easy-to-implement, practical information that had the potential to reach, and therefore help more people. While he doesn't consider himself the all-knowing "Yoda" of relationships, he still enjoys sharing the triumphs (and failures) of his love life with anyone who enjoys a good laugh or a life lesson.

When he isn't tucked away in some corner writing a literary masterpiece (or so he thinks), Bruce spends most of his time engaged in manly hobbies or being a romantic nuisance to the love of his life.

You can learn more about his writings and receive updates (and future discounts) on his books by visiting his website at: www.BruceBryans.com

Most Recommended Books by Bruce Bryans:

The 7 Irresistible Qualities Men Want In a Woman: What High-Quality Men Secretly Look For When Choosing "The One"

In *The 7 Irresistible Qualities Men Want In a Woman*, you'll find out the feminine qualities that commitment ready, high-quality men look for when choosing a long-term mate.

101 Things Your Dad Never Told You About Men: The Good, Bad, And Ugly Things Men Want And Think About Women And Relationships

In *101 Things Your Dad Never Told You About Men*, you'll learn what high-quality men want from women and what they think about love, sex, and romance. You'll learn how to seduce the man you want or captivate the man you love because you'll know exactly what makes him tick.

Make Him BEG For Your Attention: 75 Communication Secrets For Captivating Men And Getting The Love and Commitment You Deserve

In *Make Him BEG For Your Attention*, you'll discover how to talk to a man so that he listens to you, opens up to you, and gives you what you want without a fuss.

Never Chase Men Again: 38 Dating Secrets To Get The Guy, Keep Him Interested, And Avoid Dead-End Relationships

In *Never Chase Men Again*, you'll learn how to get the guy you want, train him to pursue you, and avoid dead-end or even "dead-on-arrival" relationships by being more assertive and communicating high-value to the men you date.

101 Reasons Why He Won't Commit To You: The Secret Fears, Doubts, and Insecurities That Prevent Most Men From Getting Married

In *101 Reasons Why He Won't Commit To You*, you'll learn about the most common fears, doubts, and insecurities that paralyze men and prevent them from making the leap from boyfriend to husband.

More Great Books by Bruce Bryans:

If you have a special guy in your life that could use a bit more wisdom when it comes to dating and relating with women, you should sweetly suggest that he check out some of my books. Actually, even if YOU want to learn about what guys are learning about when it comes to understanding women, peruse through my other books listed below.

Attract The Right Girl: How To Attract a High-Quality Woman, Make Her Chase You, and Get a Great Girlfriend

In *Attract The Right Girl*, you'll discover how to find and choose an amazing girlfriend (who's perfect for you) and how to spark the kind of attraction that'll lead to a long-term relationship with her.

Find Your Path: A Short Guide To Living With Purpose And Being Your Own Man…No Matter What People Think

In *Find Your Path*, you'll discover how to find your mission in life and how to become a much more self-assured man of purpose and inner conviction.

How To Be A Better Boyfriend: The Relationship Manual For Becoming Mr. Right And Making A Woman Happy

In *How To Be A Better Boyfriend*, you'll discover how to cultivate a rock-solid, mind-blowing, romantic relationship with your dream girl, and what to do to avoid all the drama, bad girlfriend behavior, and game playing that many "nice guys" often fall prey to in relationships.

How To Get Your Wife In The Mood: Quick And Easy Tips For Seducing Your Wife And Making Her BEG You For Sex

In *How To Get Your Wife In The Mood*, you'll discover the relationship secrets used by some of the most blissful couples in the world as well as romantic hacks that'll help you to get all the sex you want from your wife and make it seem like it was all HER idea.

Meet Her To Keep Her: The 10 Biggest Mistakes That Prevent Most Guys From Attracting And KEEPING An Amazing Girlfriend

In *Meet Her To Keep Her*, you'll learn the ten dating mistakes that stop most guys from attracting and keeping a 'Total 10 girlfriend' and how to overcome them.

What Women Want In A Man: How To Become The Alpha Male Women Respect, Desire, and Want to Submit To

In *What Women Want In A Man*, you'll learn how to become a high-quality, self-confident man that can naturally attract a good woman, maintain her sexual attraction to you, and keep her happy (and respectful) in a relationship.

Thank You

Before you go, I'd like to say "thank you" for purchasing my book.

I know you could have picked from dozens of books on understanding men, but you took a chance on my guide and for that I'm extremely grateful. So thanks again for downloading this book and reading all the way to the end.

Now, IF you liked this book I'm going to need your help!

Please take a moment to leave a review for this book on Amazon. Your feedback will help me to continue to write the kind of books that helps you get results. And if you so happen to love this book, then please let me know!

Made in the USA
Lexington, KY
02 December 2015